Published by Fox College of Business

© **Bryan K. Law, 2012**

All rights reserved. No part of this book may be reproduced in any form by any means, or used in any information storage and retrieval system, without the written permission of the writer.

Law, Bryan K.

Basic Feng Shui Guide

Includes index.
ISBN 978-0-9809409-8-5

1. Feng Shui   2. Geomancy – Canada

Printed in USA

Disclaimer

Fox College of Business, Bryan K. Law and every person involved in the creation of this book, disclaim any warranty as to the accuracy, completeness and currency of the contents of this book.

The adoption and application of the advice and information offered are solely the readers' responsibilities. We make no claim for absolute effectiveness and we disclaim all liability in respect of the results of any action taken or not taken in reliance upon information in this book.

This book is dedicated to my mother,

Mary, for her love and support.

About the Author – Bryan K. Law

Bryan is also the author of the best selling books *"Feng Shui 123"*, *"Real Estate; Every One Can Afford It!"*, *"Shortcut Reasoning"* and numerous articles in journals, newsletters and newspapers.

Bryan's background is deeply real estate related; author, broker, consultant, Feng Shui consultant, instructor and lease auditor – he is widely regarded as one of the foremost real estate instructors in Canada.

After 20 years of study in Feng Shui, Bryan started giving Feng Shui advice to his real estate clients. After a few years as an amateur Feng Shui consultant, Bryan found that many people still had many wrong interpretations and misunderstandings in Feng Shui. As a result, he decided to educate the public what Feng Shui is in a website, as well as to teach people the basic knowledge in Feng Shui by delivering some Feng Shui courses.

Bryan is the program creator and professor of Fox College of Business, responsible for several programs including the Higher Diploma in Feng Shui – a two-year full time program that trains students to become professional Feng Shui consultants.

Bryan K. Law BSc, LLM
FRI, CLO, CLA, REI, RPA, MVA – Residential
www.fengshui123.ca

Table of Contents

Preface

About This Book

From the excerpts of Feng Shui 123, this book was edited to assist people in choosing a good Feng Shui setting property. Whether you are a buyer, tenant or a real estate broker, you will find this book a useful and effective guide.

This is not an introduction to Feng Shui theories, or a detailed explanation of different streams and schools in Feng Shui practice. Instead, the purpose of this book is to point out the type of properties that are not good in terms of Feng Shui so that you can avoid them; or at least to know the problems and to deal with them.

Enjoy reading!

Approach Used

There were two main streams in the development of Feng Shui, one relied mainly on geography without using a compass (Form stream) and the other one relied on compass and figures (Compass stream).

Form stream came from the natural instincts of the Chinese ancestors who looked for the best place to reside by studying the geography of the area, such as topography and climate. It has to consider a wide range of area, normally within what our bare eyes can see.

Compass stream uses a compass to determine the direction is good or not, with the addition of other methods and theories, such as Bagua and Flying Stars. It has to consider the time, mainly the year, when Feng Shui is applied.

These two streams are interwoven and modern Feng Shui consultants will often use the methods from both streams to achieve the best results.

The best Feng Shui property is, of course, the one custom built with your own choice of location and style. However, as our societies are better developed and more micro-regulated than in the ancient times, it is impossible to build a home or a graveyard anywhere as we wish. We have to build houses on residential zoned lands and bury the deceased only in a licensed graveyard. Since the zoning restricts the use of our land, it makes the land use more inflexible and Feng Shui consulting is frequently limited to the micro level.

As Feng Shui was originally developed for choosing places for burial sites, its theories changed accordingly when it was applied to homes. However, many people overlook this point and apply the techniques in finding good graveyards directly to homes, which is very dangerous.

Although the methods we use are based on the both streams in Feng Shui study, we put more emphasis on the Form stream as it is independent of one's birthday (the trigram).

This kind of approach simplifies the method used in judging the Feng Shui settings so that you don't have to hassle with the calculations of trigram and the understanding of other complicated theories.

This book is designed for Feng Shui beginners to tell whether a property is good in Feng Shui setting or not.

Introduction

What is Feng Shui?

Feng Shui is the Chinese term for geomancy; a system of aesthetics with well developed theories, using geographic features, figures, directions, and the laws of nature to help one improve life by balancing the five elements - Earth, Metal, Water, Wood and Fire. Its theories rely on both Heaven (astronomy) and Earth (geography) that cover everything human beings have to deal with, both tangibly and intangibly.

Feng Shui means Wind and Water in Chinese. Its meaning emphasizes the importance of flow of Qi - both tangible and intangible. Wind can mean wind, rain, snow, sunlight, sound, magnetic fields, electromagnetic fields, infrared lights, radon gas, etc and Water can mean rivers, creeks, roads, flows of traffic and etc; they can also mean other tangible and intangible things that may not be known by us. For example, people did not know anything about radioactive substances, invisible lights and ultra high frequency sound waves one thousand years ago; but these substances did exist at that time. Feng Shui is a study on how the environment would affect people, by statistics and theories that have been developed for over four thousand years.

The Success of Feng Shui

Feng Shui is an ancient Chinese tradition with thousand years of history. There are countless examples of both successes and failures. People would, however, be skeptical that Feng Shui does not work in the western world, or even not work outside of China. There are, fortunately, many people who experienced the effect of Feng Shui and can tell you their successful stories. Ask the people around you and there will be some cases to share.

A lady told a group of people that her cousin was diagnosed with terminal cancer. One day her Chinese friend visited her cousin and told her that there was a severe Feng Shui problem in the cousin's house which had to be corrected. The cousin just corrected it by moving some furniture. Miraculously, the tumour disappeared when the cousin had the ultra-sound scan done a month later.

This was one of the miracles that happened around us, but was effective enough to show the power of Feng Shui.

How Much Can Feng Shui Help You?

First of all, let us draw an analogy. Feng Shui to a property is like a garment to a person. You have to choose suitable clothes according to your profession. If you are a businessman, you will need a suit; if you are an athlete, you will need a sport suit; if you are a diver, you will need a diving suit; etc and etc. Wearing inappropriate garment may hinder your performance, risk your career and even risk your life.

On the other hand, wearing an appropriate garment does not guarantee your success. If you are not a top athlete, wearing a sport suit will not make you a champion. However, it will not hinder your performance and will lower down your risk in injury. In other words, wearing an appropriate garment can maximize your performance and give you the biggest protection.

Feng Shui has the same functions to properties. Having a good Feng Shui can boost your luck; you will be able to maximize your return. However, it is not a guarantee of success; for example, you cannot just sit and wait for your luck to come without doing anything.

Can Feng Shui Bring Bad Luck?

Definitely! You may have good Feng Shui
and can have bad Feng Shui too. Having
bad Feng Shui is like eating poisoned foods
which can bring you sickness or even
death.

Some Feng Shui practitioners like to use
special settings of Feng Shui in order to
maximize the effects. Such settings require
complex and accurate calculations of one's
trigram, directions and flying stars. Since
there is a high risk, only people with
challenging goals will take such risk.
Ordinary people should not take such an
approach as the risk is too high and it may
not be worth to take it.

Moreover, Feng Shui relies on the
universe, and righteousness is a
foundation of it. One cannot use Feng Shui
to assist illegal activities or to cover
them. A famous Feng Shui master was
hired by an accused to assist him in
defending the prosecution by putting up a
special Feng Shui setting; however the

accused was eventually convicted as there were tons of evidences to prove his participation in that illegal activity. This is an example to show Feng Shui does not help people in that way.

Contemporary Feng Shui

It is undeniable that Feng Shui is an ancient subject. As society has developed and people have evolved, it is necessary to make Feng Shui practices adapt to our new society. For example, there was no electric tower, no flyover and no subway one hundred years ago; but we have to deal with these Feng Shui problems now. This is how the term *Contemporary Feng Shui* comes.

The fact is: our society did not change overnight. Feng Shui has been developed, expanded, modified and improved to fit the changes of society in the past four thousand years. It keeps on changing everyday and it is contemporary already. If you study the Feng Shui nowadays and compare with those in the ancient books, you will find that many theories have already been added to it. The principles, however, are still the same.

Some geomancers copied some theories from Feng Shui without knowing its principles, added their own stuff to it and called it *contemporary Feng Shui*. That is unacceptable. Some geomancers said it was not good to place a single lamp post in front of a bed, as it meant 'One Night Stand'; which was not good for getting or maintaining a stable relationship.

They simply used the 'homophonic' words – 'One Light Stand' to 'One Night Stand'. Many people would find this funny and accept the interpretation of it. It is not sure if such kind of geomancy works or not, but definitely it is not Feng Shui.

Did the Chinese speak English four thousand years ago as their mother tongue? Did the term 'One Night Stand' appear four thousand years ago? Definitely not! There is no way such kind of geomancy to be part of Feng Shui.

You may copy a Chinese character, use it as a pattern, and write it in different fonts. You can even change the character into a diagram in a way that the diagram is no longer a Chinese character. People may admire this as a fine art. However, you cannot use such diagrams to write a Chinese essay. No one in the world will be able to understand such essay except you. It is because the 'characters' you used are no longer Chinese characters; they are just some 'diagrams' invented by you.

The same logic applies to some of the so-called contemporary Feng Shui promoters. Feng Shui is not a fine art and cannot be changed that way. Those promoters just used a small portion of Feng Shui concepts and called their new inventions 'contemporary Feng Shui'.

Contemporary Feng Shui is not a phrase used to twist the meaning of Feng Shui; it should be genuine Feng Shui with modern applications.

To be fair to everyone - the genuine Feng Shui practitioners, believers and general public, those contemporary Feng Shui without the support of full Feng Shui principles should not be called Feng Shui. They should be called Geomancy Design, or Contemporary Geomancy, or any other name, but NOT Feng Shui.

Does Feng Shui Work in North America?

In order to answer this question, we have to know the development of Feng Shui in China and its major theory used.

Feng Shui was developed in the Central China. Most of the Feng Shui techniques are based on the Bagua. Each direction in the Bagua is assigned to one of the Five Elements. North belongs to Water, South belongs to Fire, Northeast and Southwest belong to Earth, West and Northwest belong to Metal, East and Southeast belong to Wood.

Such assignments are in fact based on the geographic nature of China. China is in the north hemisphere so that the northern part of it is cold and the southern part is hot. This explains why North is Water (being cool) and South is Fire (being hot). Therefore, only the countries in north hemisphere have the same nature. That is, both the USA and Canada fit these characteristics.

Both the Northeast and Southwest part of China are consisting of high mountains, including the famous Mount Everest in Tibet and the Changbai Mountain in Northeast China. This is why Northeast and Southwest are Earth (have many mountains)

Xinjiang is located in the west and northwest parts of China, where it has large deposits of minerals. This is why West and Northwest are Metal (being metal mines).

The eastern and southeast parts of China are the major agricultural areas. This explains why East and Southeast parts are Wood (have many plants).

I cannot say other countries or regions do not have such characteristics, but I can say that at least the Province of Ontario fits all of those characteristics and I am lucky to be here to apply the Feng Shui.

Section I – Exterior Feng Shui

We have to know that a home may be good for you, but it may not be good for me. It is because our birth year may not be the same (to be exact, our trigram may not be the same). Different trigram needs different direction (the direction that the home is facing).

Without a detailed study of trigram and the knowledge of Bagua, it is difficult to tell whether the facing is good to you or not. This is why we will study the Form Stream – the appearance of the property instead of using trigrams.

The followings are the common bad Feng Shui settings; you should avoid from buying those properties with such settings. However, if your home has one (or more) of the following settings; don't worry, there are solutions for them (see my previous book *Feng Shui 123*).

Location of Building

You should always pay attention to the surroundings of the property before buying it. It is better to buy a home with safe and sound Feng Shui without worrying how to rectify the problems than buying a house with Feng Shui challenges and getting the best solutions to fix them.

However, no matter how knowledgeable you are, it is unlikely you can find a home with perfect Feng Shui. While you can renovate the interior of your home, the surrounding environment is out of your control. It is therefore crucial to check the surrounding area before buying a home.

If your home is close to a hospital, graveyard or funeral home, there will be too much Yin in your area; which is not good. It will be worse if you have a small family (not enough Yang in the house).

Chimney Nearby

A tall chimney is a type of Sha (Figure 1); especially the big stand alone chimneys used in heavy industries, power generation plants, and incinerators.

The shape of a chimney is a tall pole, representing Wood. The physical nature of a chimney is extremely hot, representing Fire.

Putting these two characteristics together would mean a large burning wood, which is extremely Fire.

Even though the chimney is not close to your home, but if you can see such a chimney from the outside or inside of your home; then the Sha will affect you. Of course, the closer is the worse.

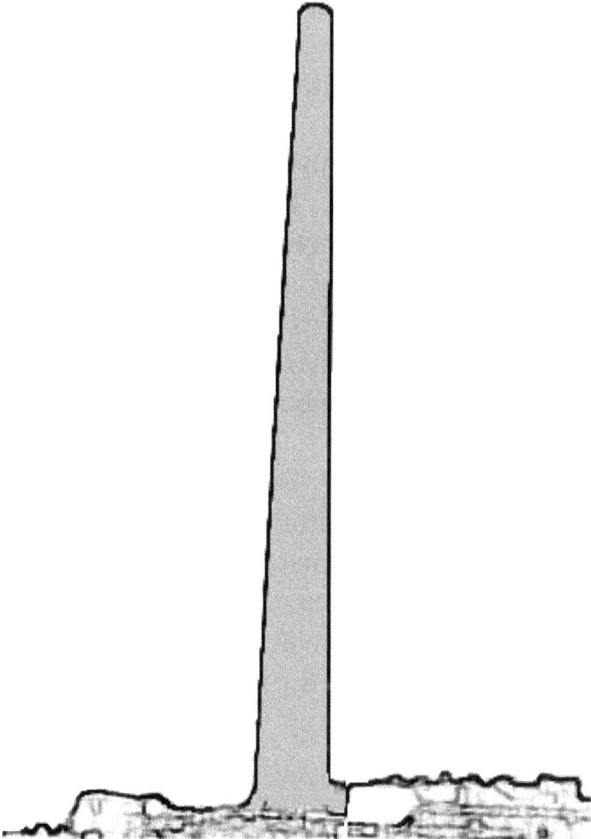

Figure 1

A Chimney is like a large piece of burning log, which is a strong Sha

Curved Road

Buildings sitting opposite of a curved road are facing an Anti-Bow Sha (Figure 2), which is not good. On the contrary, if the building is sitting on the interior side of the curved road (Figure 3), it is good. The building is like being protected by an arm; and the Qi will arrive calmly.

For a building that is sitting opposite of a curved road, the Qi will be too strong and the building is like being but by a saber (the anti-bow shaped road).

The worst situation of a curved road is when there is a streetlight pole or a tree on it (Figure 4). It is like an arrow on a bow, shooting at the building.

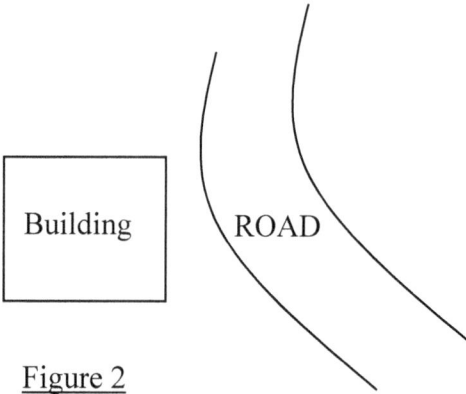

Figure 2

A building on the opposite side of a curved road is not good.

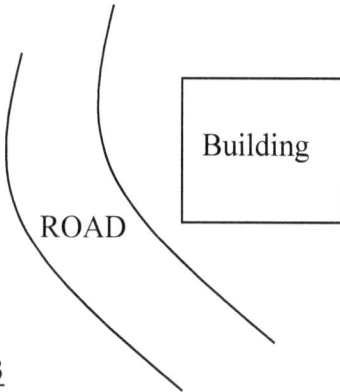

Figure 3

A building on the interior of a curved road is good.

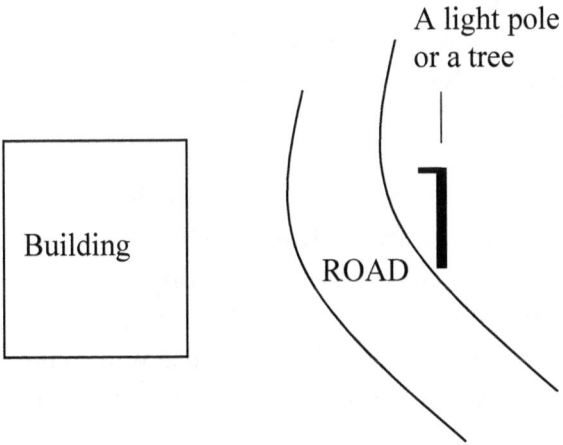

A light pole or a tree

Building

ROAD

<u>Figure 4</u>

The streetlight pole is like an arrow on a bow, shooting the building.

Elevator

If you live in a high-rise building and the door of your unit is directly facing an elevator door, it will make you lose money and cause bad health.

A unit that is directly facing an elevator will have too many traffic. The elevator opens and closes, people coming out from the elevator or waiting outside your door to get into the elevator; all these will make a noisy environment which is not good in Feng Shui too.

Since the elevator is right outside your unit, it makes your entrance a meeting place. Such a high traffic area outside your home creates not only noise, but dust and garbage.

Extended Upper Level

Some houses have extended upper levels and some buildings are also built in the shape as a flag (Figure 5). Such a shape is like standing with one foot, which represent unstable and unsafe Feng Shui.

If you see such a kind of building, the best idea will be to not move in.

<u>Figure 5</u>

Building with lower level(s) narrower than the upper level(s)

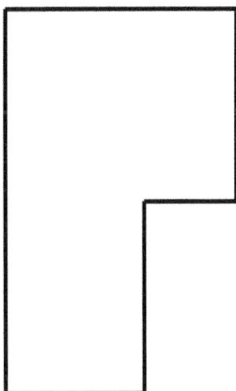

Facing a Sharp Edge

Sharp branches of a tree pointing to your home are not good, nor are the sharp edges of other buildings nearby (Figure 6). They produce Sha that point to your home.

The edge of another building is a Sha; it is like a knife pointing to you. If it is far away, the effect will not be significant. If it is very close, such as two high-rise buildings close to each other, the Sha will be very strong.

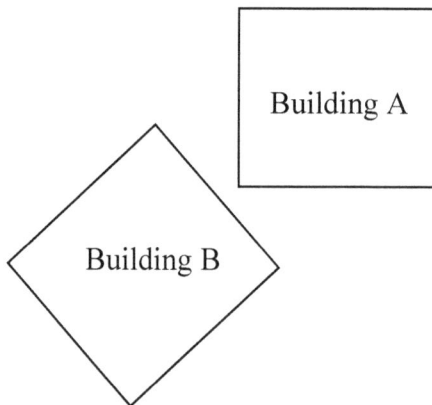

Figure 6

Building B is facing the sharp point of Building A. People who live in that side of Building B are facing a Sha.

Front Door Directly Facing a Road

If the front door of a house is directly facing a road (Figure 7), the best idea will be to not buy it.

The strong Qi on the road is pointing directly toward the house; like a river rushes to the house. It is one of the worst settings in Feng Shui.

All the three situations illustrated in Figure 7 are not good. However, if there is an island at the end of a cal-de-sac (Figure 8), it is a good location. The island will serve as a buffer and make the Qi become calm and mild. The Qi becomes good and stay in front of the house.

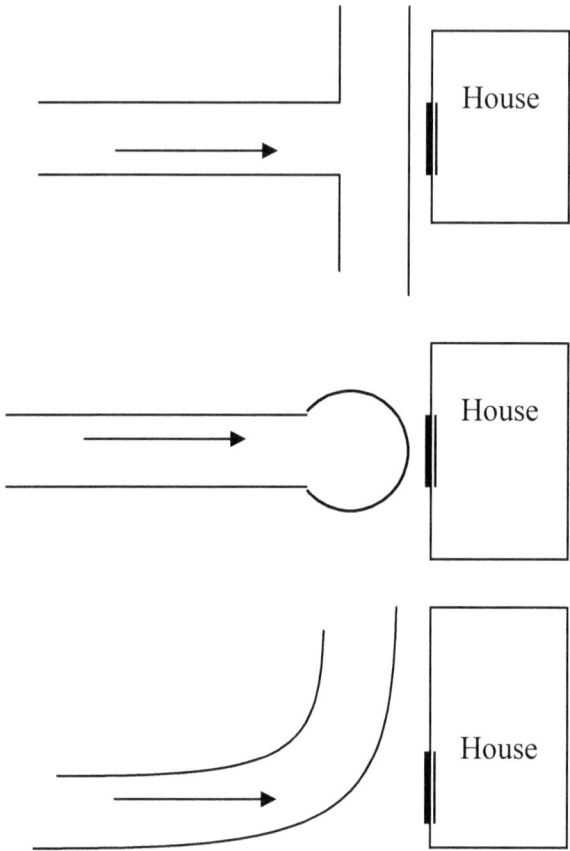

Figure 7

All the houses above are directly facing a road.

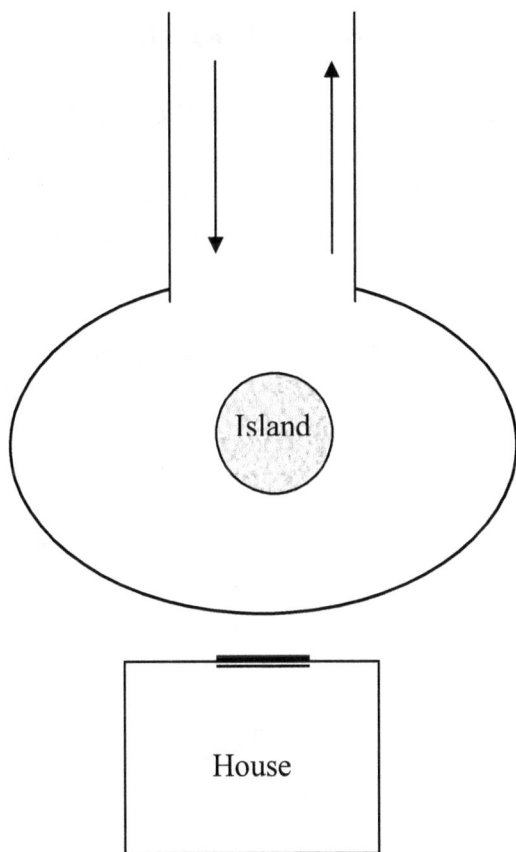

Figure 8

The island serves as a buffer to make the Qi calm and mild.

31

Ocean Views and Lake Views

Homes with magnificent ocean views or lake views are always welcome, especially for million dollar homes. They are, however, not necessarily good Feng Shui homes to us.

If the view is a small lake or part of the sea with hills beyond the water (Figure 9), it is a very good Feng Shui.

Figure 9

An ocean view (lake view) with boundaries

Since water represents wealth and there is abundance of water in the sea (lake); that means it is a wealthy home. If the water is trapped by the hills; that will mean you can retain your wealth.

On the contrary, if the view is facing an open ocean or open lake (Figure 10), the water is too vigorous and is not good in Feng Shui. The Qi is simply too strong; and when the waves hit the shores, the strong Qi attacks you. When the water recedes back to the ocean (lake), it will bring away your luck and wealth.

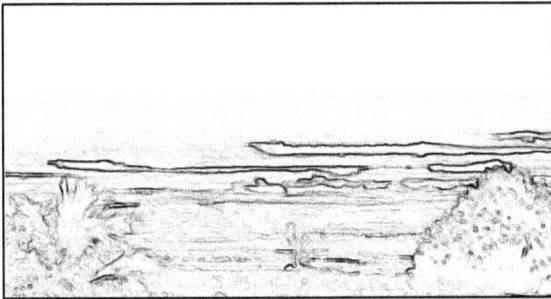

Figure 10

A view facing an open ocean (open lake)

If there is an island in the centre of the water but there are open waters on the sides (Figure 11), the waters in both sides will still bring your luck away.

Figure 11

An island in the middle part of the view

Rocky Hills or Bald Slopes

Hills and Mountains should be green – covered by grass and trees. They represent healthy and wealthy environment for residents nearby.

Rocky hills represent ominousness and bald slopes represent decadence. They are not good Feng Shui, especially when they are at the back of your home.

Psychologically, we love to view green fields instead of brown fields. Moreover, green colour is good for our eyes and the reason for having bald slopes may be contamination; which not good for our health if we live nearby.

Stand Alone High-rise Building

We have many high-rise buildings in downtown areas nowadays; but in some areas, there may be only one high-rise building in that neighbourhood (Figure 12).

A stand alone high-rise building creates a Lonely Sha; people living inside this kind of building will end up having a lonely life. Either the residents will be single for life, or their children will leave them and seldom visit them, or they will simply have no friends.

One thing that must be mentioned is that all people who can see such a building in their homes will also be affected the Sha; the effect is lighter though.

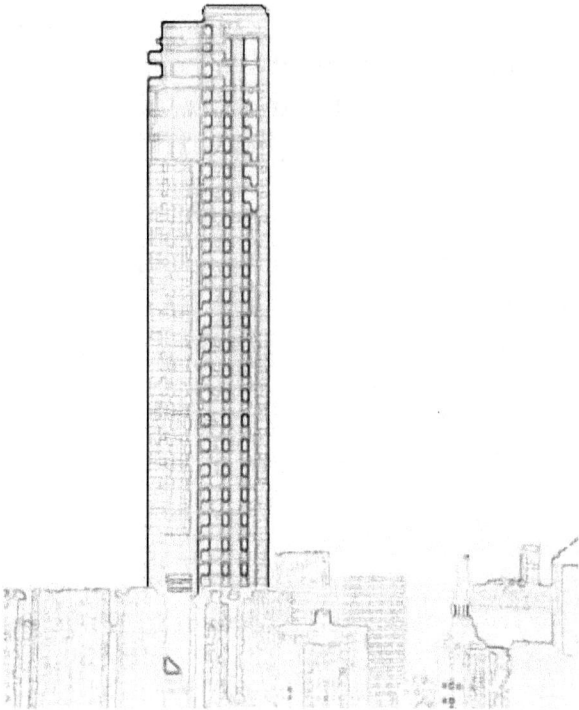

Figure 12

Stand alone high-rise buildings cause loneliness

Subway Tunnel Underneath

It was inconceivable that in ancient time that there would be a tunnel underneath your home that might run for miles. There were, however, hollow grounds and underground creeks that would weaken the foundation of houses.

Modern technology can strengthen the foundations of buildings so that subway tunnels can pass through the underground of high-rise buildings without worrying about affecting the foundations. However, the Sha in Feng Shui is still there since it is a hollow shape underneath a home.

Sometimes we have to sacrifice our health for convenience. We know it from the fast food restaurants.

Two Buildings That Are Too Close

When two multi-level buildings are built too closely, they create an Axed Sha (Figure 13). In ancient time, such kind of Sha would not be strong as the buildings were not high. Now, we have the skyscrapers in many cities and some of them are twin buildings. These create very strong Axed Sha.

When two skyscrapers are closely built, the Axed Sha is strong and the damage can be very significant. It may take years for the damages to be caused, but the damages can be substantial and even fatal.

For buildings with strong Axed Sha, it does not matter if it is an apartment or an office building; the best idea is not to move in.

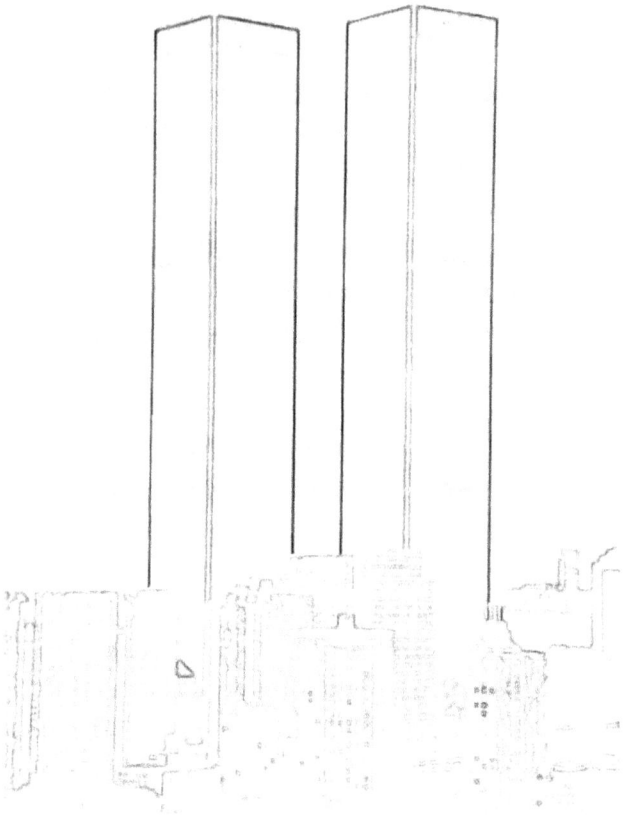

<u>Figure 13</u>

Two high-rise buildings with a narrow gap,
the shape is like one building cut into two
by an axe from the sky.

40

Section II – Interior Feng Shui

Beams

Beams (Figure 14) on the ceiling are not good Feng Shui, they represent pressure and burden on you.

You should never sleep or sit directly under a beam, as it presses on you and will make you tire and hinder your luck.

Figure 14

A beam represents pressure and burden.

Bedroom Light

It is more convenient to have a ceiling light in our bedroom, but a floor light or table light is better in Feng Shui.

Having a light in the bedroom ceiling is like having something above you press on you when you sleep. If possible, it is better to use floor lights, table lights or wall lights. If a ceiling light must be used, you should pay attention to the shape of the light.

The bedroom is a place for rest so the light should be stable in nature. Therefore, bedroom ceiling lights should be square or rectangular in shape, as such shapes represent stability.

A more important point about ceiling light fixtures is that there should be no sharp point coming from the shed or the frame. Any sharp tip pointing to your bed is not good and should be avoided.

Chandelier

A chandelier is similar to a beam, which presses on you. Chandeliers also have sharp tips, which are not good.

If the chandelier is in the dining room, you should put a dining table under the chandelier for support even if that dinning room is not used. One more benefit of it is to prevent people from hurting their heads when passing through that room as the dining chandelier is usually hung at a lower position than a chandelier in a hallway or foyer area.

In all cases, you should not place any sofa under it and should not sit right under any chandelier.

The foyer is the best location for a chandelier as you will not stay in the foyer for a long period of time so the effect will not be long and will not be significant.

Corners and Sharp Edges

There are columns, air ducts and furniture that may have corners or sharp edges. These edges are not good in Feng Shui as they are Sha pointing to you (Figure 15).

Round tables are better than rectangular or square ones as round tables have no corners. Similarly, round columns are better than square ones and so on.

You should not put your bed or seat to face such a sharp edge, at least, not facing your head.

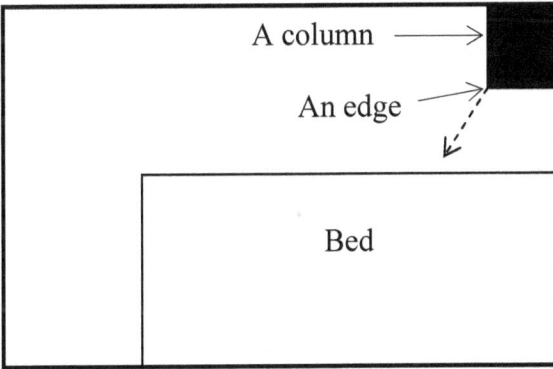

A column

An edge

Bed

Figure 15

An edge pointing to a bed

The Entrance Door

The entrance is the mouth of your home and is one of the most important parts. Entrances should not be blocked as the Qi (wealth) has to enter our homes freely from the outside through the entrances.

On the other hand, the Qi should not be too strong. For apartment units, it is not uncommon that the entrance door is directly opposite of a bedroom door or a window (Figure 16). This will make the Qi rushing in and it causes problem.

Similarly, an entrance door should not be in line with a back door, such as a patio door.

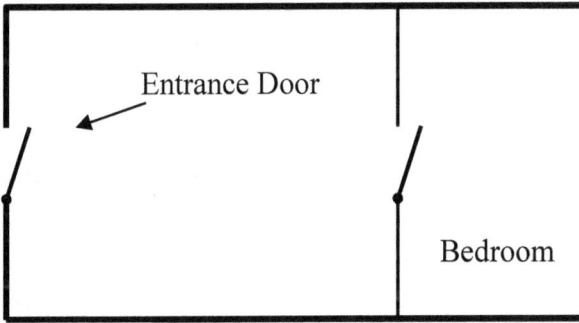

Entrance Door

Bedroom

Figure 16

Entrance door is inline with a bedroom door.

Main Entrance Facing the Stairway

It is quite common in North America to have the main entrance of a house directly face the stairway.

More and more people now know this setting is a bad Feng Shui as the Wealth of your home will slide from the stairs to the outside through the main entrance.

If there is a door sill in the main entrance that is three inches or higher, then it will help you to prevent the wealth from escaping by blocking it on the ground.

If your home has no door sill or it is less than three inches high; then there is nothing to block the wealth from running out to the outside.

Marble Floor

Marble tiles are the 'standard' floorings for million dollar homes. Marble was extensively used for sculptures and as a building material in many countries. You can find it in many churches, temples and monuments.

In ancient China and some other countries, marble was used only in mausoleums and tombs. To be exact, marble was used for only Yin (the deceased) residence. Therefore, marble is not suitable for use in our homes as it is too Yin to have it.

You may have a small portion of home that is made with marble, such as a marble window sill or marble countertop. However, a marble floor or a marble wall is too Yin and should be avoided.

Mirrors

Mirrors are in fact Feng Shui tools. We
have convex mirrors, flat mirrors and
concave mirrors to be used for different
purposes.

Mirrors are used to collect, divert or reflect
Qi, both good and bad. Placing a mirror at
home without knowing its function and
the nature of the spot is dangerous, as the
mirror may disturb the Qi, attract or reflect
bad Qi to you.

In general, all mirrors should be covered at
home and should only be uncovered when
they are used. The only exception may be
in the bathroom, as bathroom is the place
where we will stay the least time and it is
more convenient for modern people to
have big mirrors fixed in their bathrooms.
However, a wall to wall mirror is too big
and should be avoided.

You should never place a mirror in a
bedroom facing your bed. It will disturb
your Qi and your sleep too. It will also

affect your luck. Placing a mirror to face a door is also not recommended.

Similarly, television and computer monitors should also not be placed in bedrooms. If you want to, they should be covered or placed in a cabinet with a door.

Missing Corner(s)

The best shape of a house or an apartment unit is a square. The worst type is an irregular shape with the four missing corners of a square or a round one without corners.

A home with one or more missing corners (Figure 17) represents its lack of some luck and the resident in the corresponding Bagua position will have problems (Figure 18).

For example, a house with a missing corner at the east means the eldest son will have bad luck. If the family has no son, it will mean the couple will not have son but daughters.

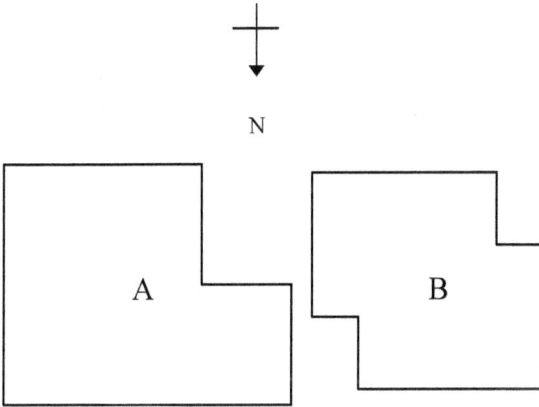

Figure 17

House A is missing the south-west corner
and House B is missing the north-east and
south-west corners. Both are not good.

South East	South	South West
Eldest Daughter	Middle Daughter	Mother
East		West
Eldest Son		Youngest Daughter
North East	North	North West
Youngest Son	Middle Son	Father

Figure 18

Each direction in Bagua represents a person at home.

Nails and Hanging Hooks

We put nails and hooks on walls and ceilings to hang frames, flower pots or other stuff. When they are not used, you should take them out to make the wall (ceilings) flat.

As we have discussed before, having a sharp edge pointing to you is not good. Nails and hooks without anything to be hung on are sharp objects, just like knives on the wall, pointing to you everyday.

If you let those nails and hooks stay on walls without covering them (hanging something on them), they will create bad Qi and point to you.

You should take out the nail or hook whenever you don't need it.

Posters, Statues and Ornaments

Unlike offices and other workplaces, our home is the place we rest and thus should be calm in nature.

Posters and statues with armies, fighters, vampires and all other scary or violent themes are not suitable at home. They will make the residents hot-tempered or even violent.

Nude posters and statues are not suitable either, as they will spoil the spousal relationship. If the occupant is single, they will make it impossible for the occupant to find a companion.

Some people like paintings of wild animals such as tigers, wolves or lions. These animals are offensive in nature, so they are not recommended for homes. If you really want to hang such kind of paintings at home, you should pay attention to the position of the animals. They should be facing the outside or on the ground (you will see their backs instead of their faces) so that they will not be able to attack you.

Ornaments such as knives, guns and deer head mounts are not suitable for homes. They are too Yang and may bring violence to your home. You should remove all these kinds of ornaments to calm down your home. However, if you belong to the Yang professions such as the police force, army or butcher, this kind of ornament may increase your Yang so that you can do your job better. However, they may still be harmful to other family members. You should put such ornament in your workplace instead of your home, unless you live alone.

Stairs

Stairs provide us access from one floor to
another floor. It also provides a pathway
for Qi. Therefore, stairs are very important
in Feng Shui.

It is not good to have a circular stairway,
because it is too curved that it will stir up
all the Qi in your house and make you
restless.

Stair should not be in the centre of a house,
as its stirring force is the strongest. Just
imagine when you stir a glass of water; the
centre is always the most vigorous.
Having a circular stair in the centre of a
house is the worst.

The Scarlett O'Hara stair is elegant but,
again, elegant items may not good in Feng
Shui.

The design of the Scarlett O'Hara stair is a
Y shaped stairway with a wide section at
the bottom and splitting at the middle,
going to two opposite directions above.

This kind of design is in fact splitting the family members into to two different directions. It will make the people living there have a sense of separation and eventually a lack of communications.

All types of stairs that split at the end have the same kind of effect on the residents.

Stove

The direction of your stove is very important. It should not be facing the back of your house (Figure 19). That is, when you cook, you should not be facing the front of your house. You should move the stove to the other three directions.

The stove should not be placed next to the sink, as the water faucet belongs to the element Water and the stove belongs to the element Fire. Water and Fire cannot be put together.

The stove should not be directly exposed to sunlight. You should close the blind to prevent sunlight from shining directly on the stove.

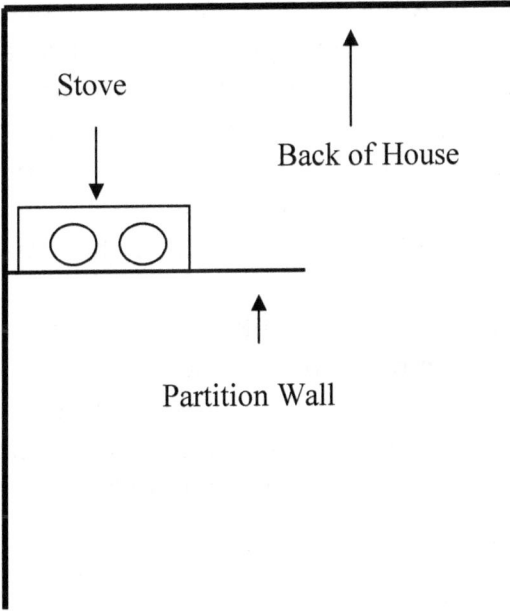

Stove

Back of House

Partition Wall

Figure 19

The stove is 'facing' the back of the
house, which is not good.

Swimming Pool

In North America, many house owners like to have a swimming pool in their backyard. Having a pool in the backyard is a bad Feng Shui, because we need a solid ground (preferable some trees) as a support at our back. A swimming pool is a hollow ground and gives no support to the house.

Just imagine it is just like you are working on something outdoors, and there is a pool behind you; you are 'trapped' and can easily fall into the pool. It is therefore not recommended to have a pool in the backyard.

A Swimming pool should be kidney shaped or in the shape of a figure '8', as water in such shapes represent luck and wealth. Having a rectangular shaped swimming pool is the worst.

Two Entrance Doors

Some homes have two entrance doors, especially those that are combined units. Some people like to buy two adjacent semi-detached houses and make it a large detached home. All these homes with two entrance doors will have the effect of separation.

Like the Scarlett O'Hara stairway, a home with two entrance doors will split the family members into two different directions. It will make the people living there have a sense of separation and eventually a lack of communications. The relationships among them will be spoiled.

Conclusion

The Feng Shui setting of a house may be perfect for you, but it may not be perfect for everyone in the house. When there is a big family residing in the same house, it is impossible to set the Feng Shui to fit all of the family members. The reason is that their trigrams (based on their birthday) are not the same. It is therefore impossible to set the Feng Shui to fit all of them.

However, all the issues discussed above will apply to everyone in the house. They are independent of the birthdays of the residents. This is because this book use only Form stream to apply Feng Shui and Form stream is independent to one's birthday (the trigram).

For a detailed Feng Shui setting, you should hire a competent Feng Shui consultant to audit it for you. Now, online Feng Shui auditing is available to most of the areas in the world, thanks to the GPS and other hi-tech tools available in the Internet.

www.ingramcontent.com/pod-product-compliance
Lightning Source LLC
Chambersburg PA
CBHW071021040426
42443CB00007B/889